I0467386

# Birth Mandala Colouring Book

## By April Wood

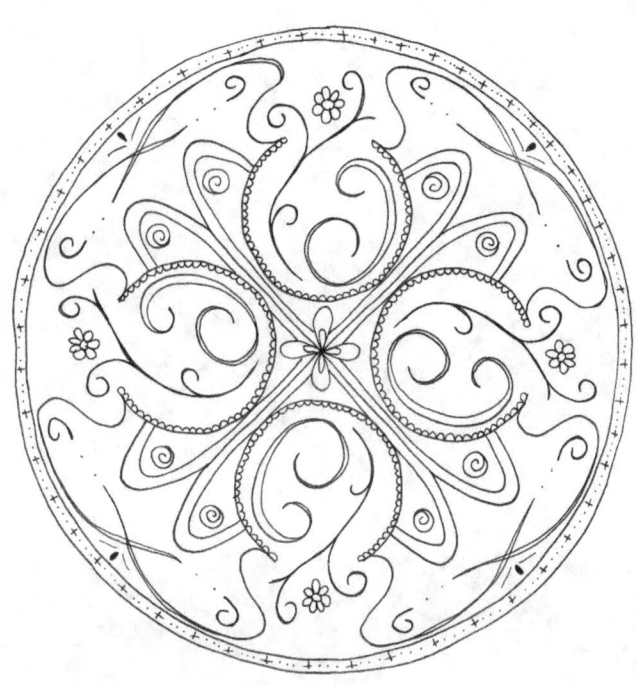

# Introduction

Colouring in is a wonderfully relaxing way for many people to spend time. By colouring in these beautiful mandalas you will be able to spend time connecting with your baby while simultaneously creating gorgeous artwork.

Many women like to use the coloured in mandalas in their birthing space to help them focus and give them inner strength during their births.
I have given a short description of why I created each of the included mandalas, however if you look at one and it has a different meaning to you- that is completely ok!
I have provided you with the basic images, they are now yours to fill with colour, life, and joy.

There is a blank mandala at the end of this colouring book which will allow you make your own mandala if you so choose.

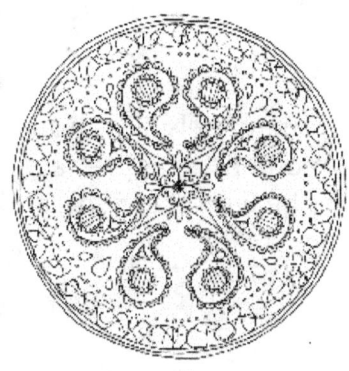

## Conception

This mandala is full of life, it represents the dividing of cells and growth of a new life at the moment of conception, full of potential, beauty and love.

## Gestation

Conception through to full term, each circle represents a month of pregnancy.

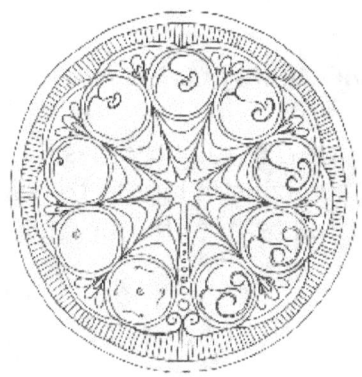

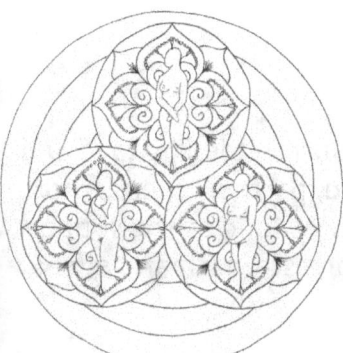

## Motherhood

From maiden to pregnant to motherhood. It is a cycle that every mother goes through, each with its own unique sets of challenges, accomplishments and rewards.

## Blooming Slowly

The lotus is a common symbol used in relation to birthing and new life. Here a bud is shown to slowly bloom into a fully open flower, this could either symbolize dilating and blooming through your labour, or blooming into a full pregnancy- the choice is yours!

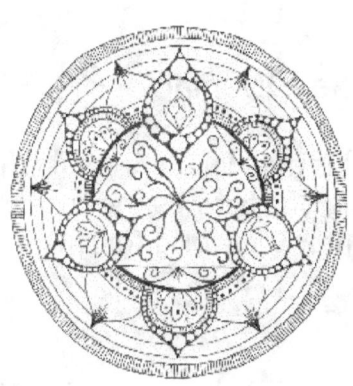

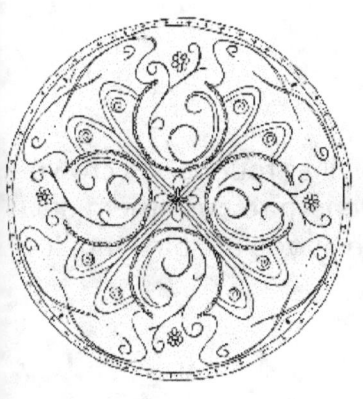

## Pregnant Sisters

Here four pregnant women are sitting with their arms around each other as they give and find support on the journey they are embarking on together. As a pregnant woman it is so important to ensure you have the right support around you for the whole journey ahead.

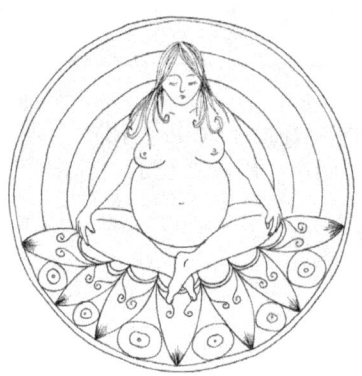

## Suspended time

The end of pregnancy is often a time where a woman feels like all she is doing is waiting. This is a reminder to take a moment to appreciate this time, embrace the calm and beauty of being heavily pregnant, and relish the time before you meet this beautiful new baby.

## Blooming Lotus

A lotus in full bloom is full of beauty and peace. It is a great image for visualizing in labour to help dilation. It is also representative of a woman at full term of her pregnancy.

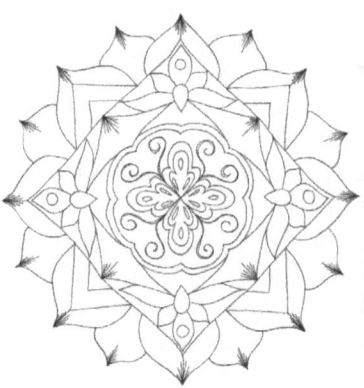

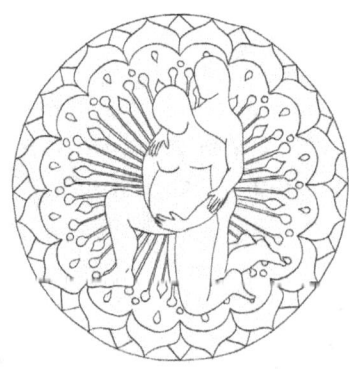

## The Support

It is so important that every pregnant woman is surrounded by love and support. The person supporting may be a husband, partner, friend, mother, doula, midwife, doctor, sister or someone else. As long as the support person is there for the mother,  to provide comfort, strength and encouragement.

## The Opening

This mandala represents the opening required to birth, and the crowning of a baby as they come down through the birth canal and is about the enter the world for their first breath of air

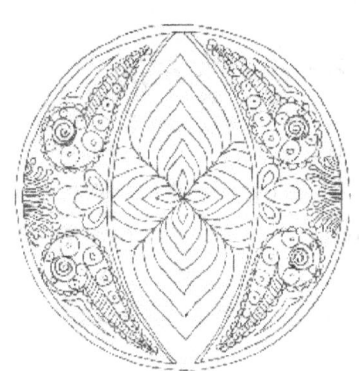

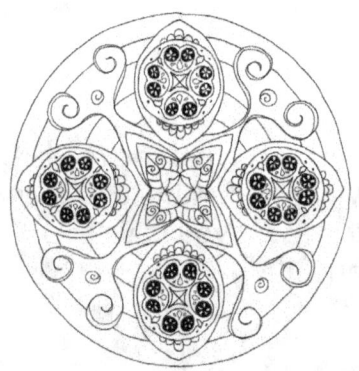

## Strong Woman

Four women showing how strong they are, as well as four babies crowning after their mothers have used their inner strength to push them out. This is a reminder to draw on that inner strength as you are birthing, it is within us all.

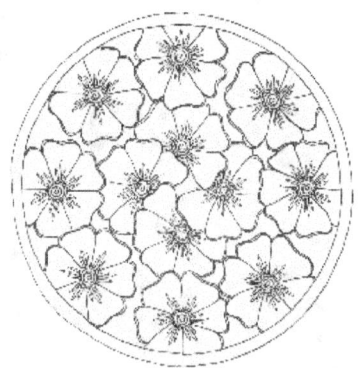

## Full Bloom

A bowl full of flowers in full bloom, full of life, about to give birth, opening and dilating, pure beauty and joy. Flowers are synonymous with birth and life

## Common-unity

Here 8 people are banded together holding hands in a show of community. Parenting is a time when we should be able to rely on those around us to help support us in the tough times, and help us navigate our journey.

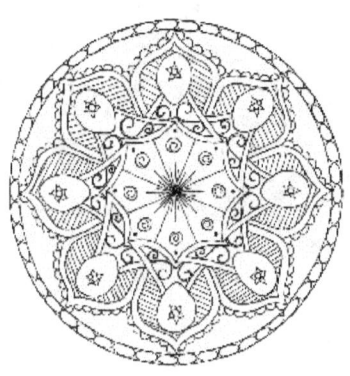

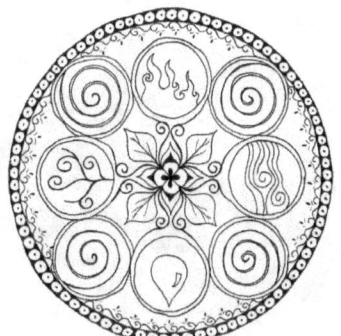

## The Elements

Five elements- fire, air, water, wood, and earth (centre) all come together to create life and energy

## Dream Catcher

This image represents capturing all of a pregnant woman's dreams and aspirations, clearing her fears and bad dreams, and giving her hope, happiness and joy for the coming birth

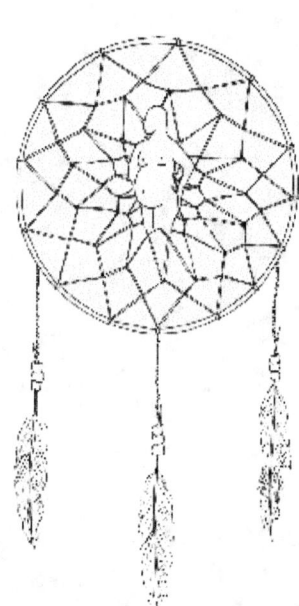

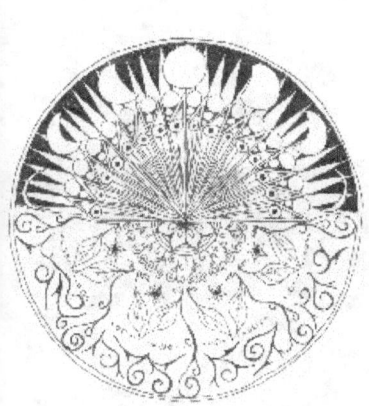

## Opposites attract

In this busy mandala it represents night and day, growth and death, man and woman. It is a depiction of natures organization to work as a living organism to bring forth life.

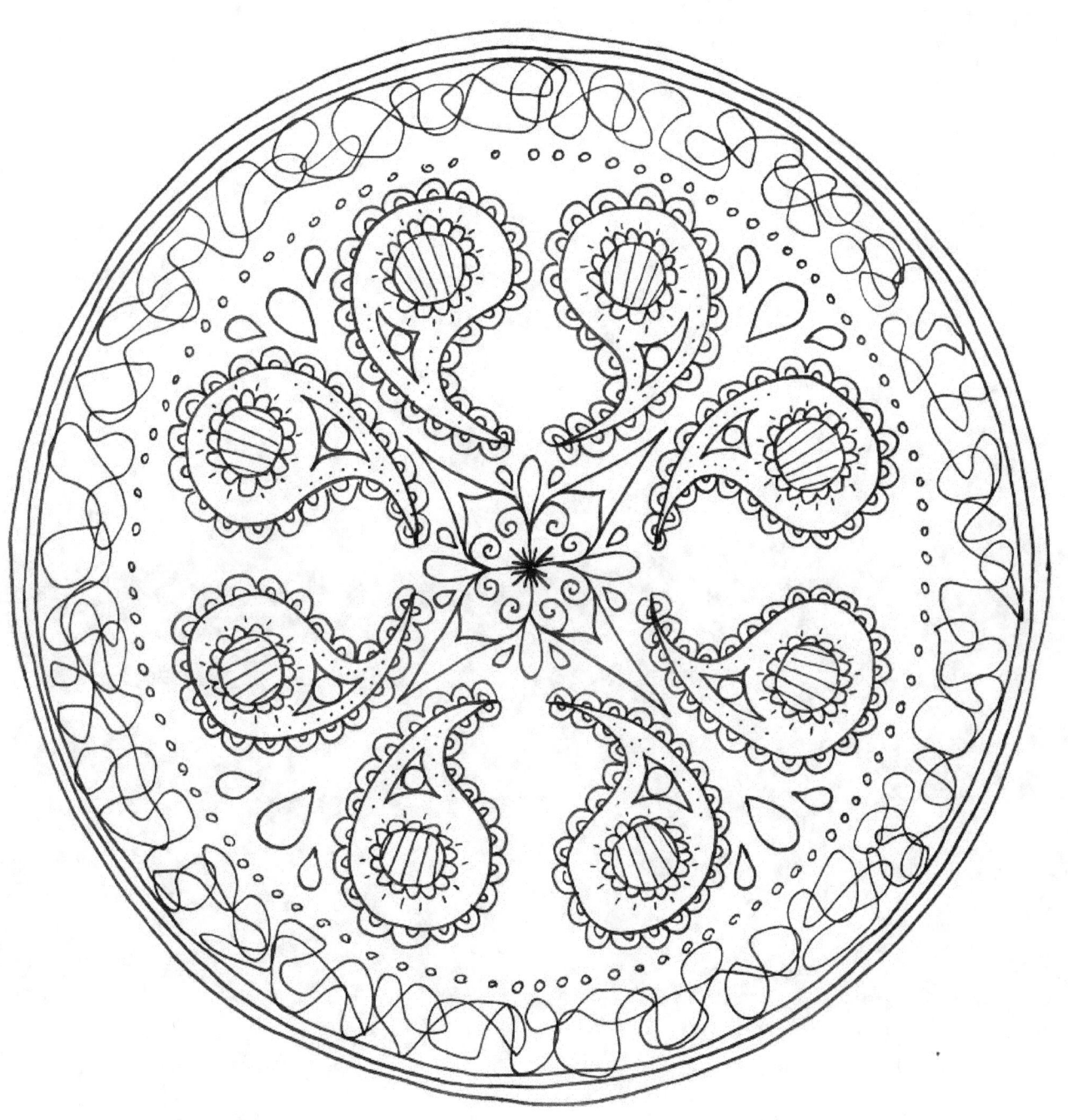

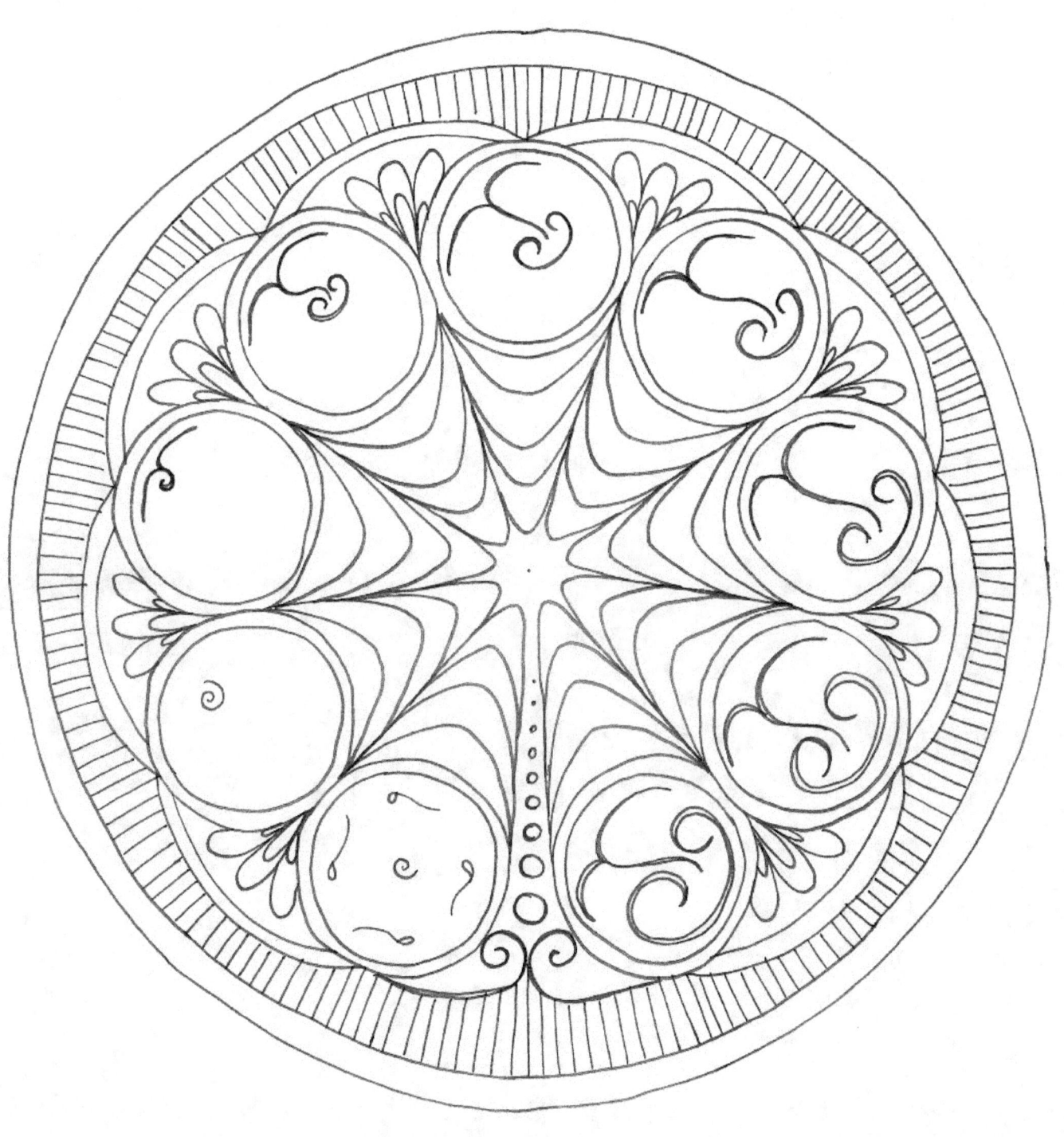

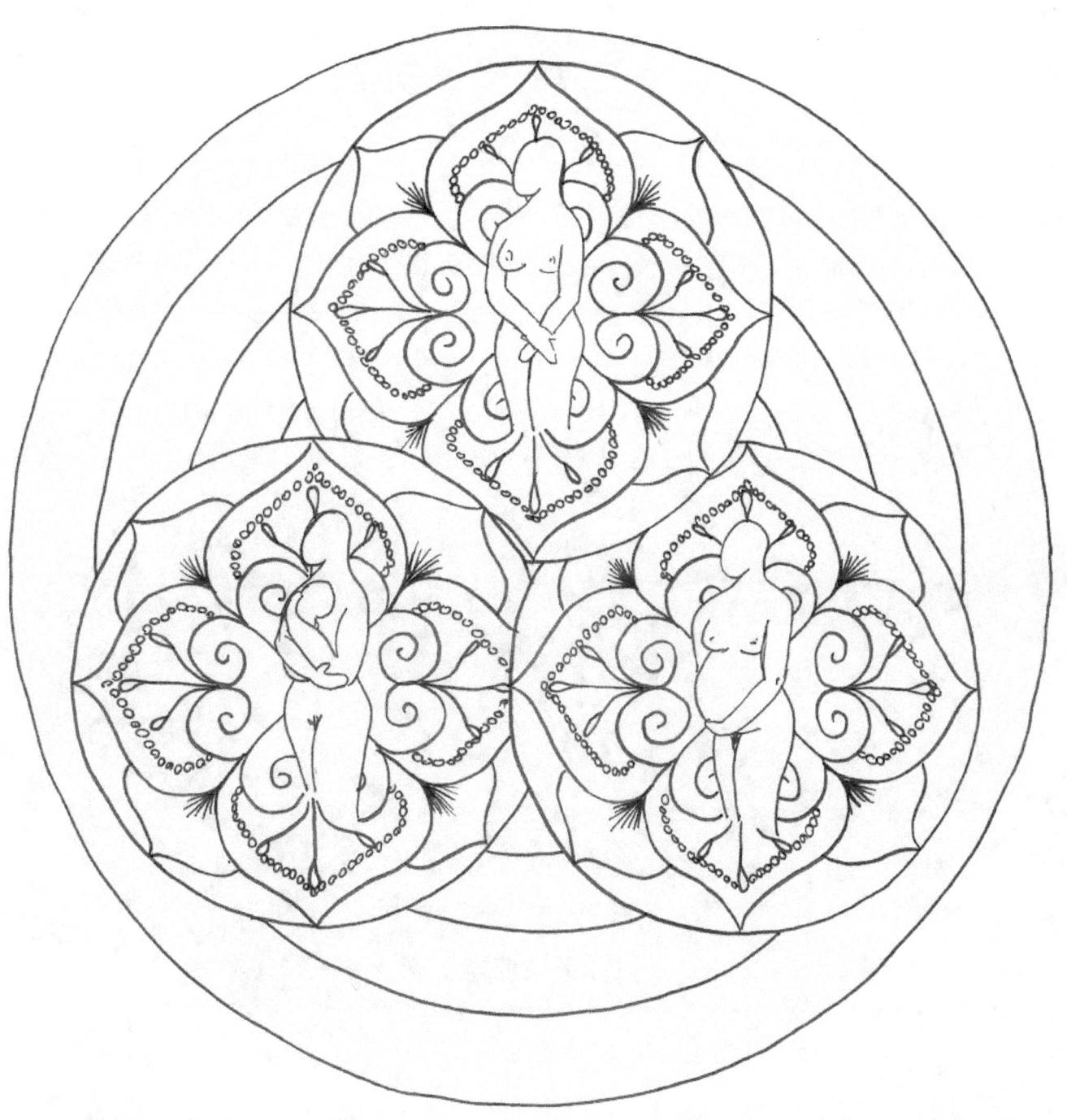

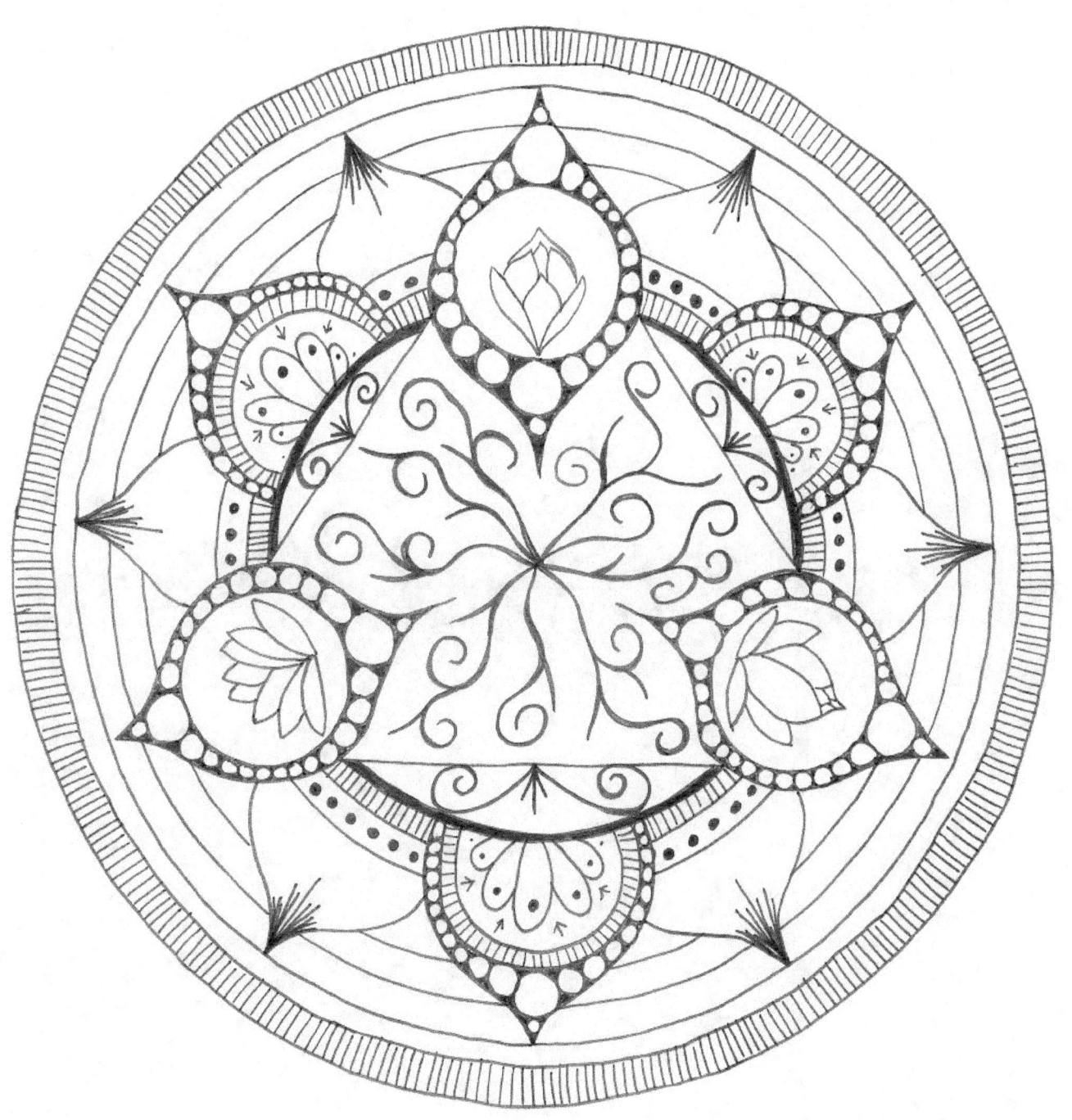

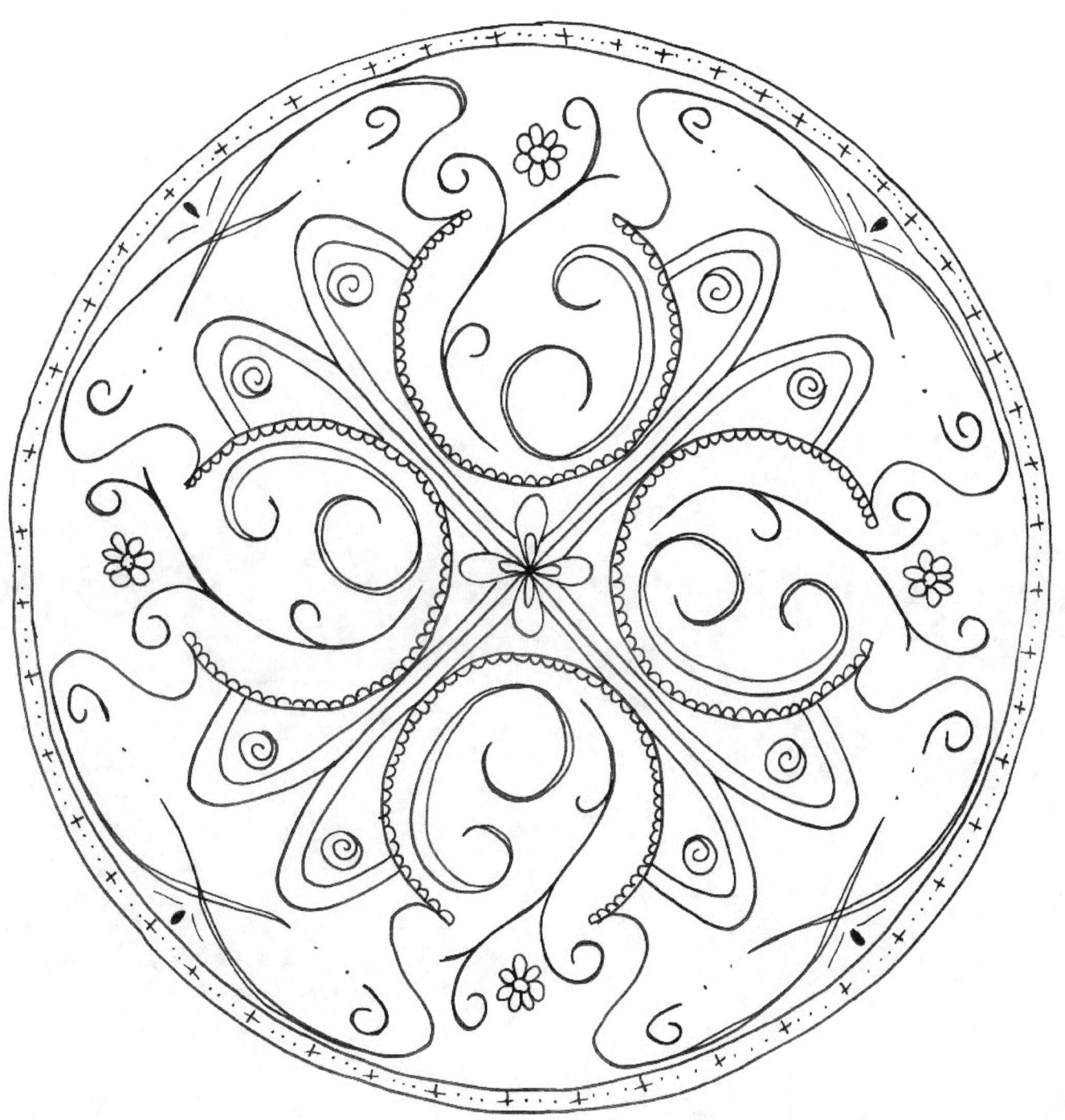

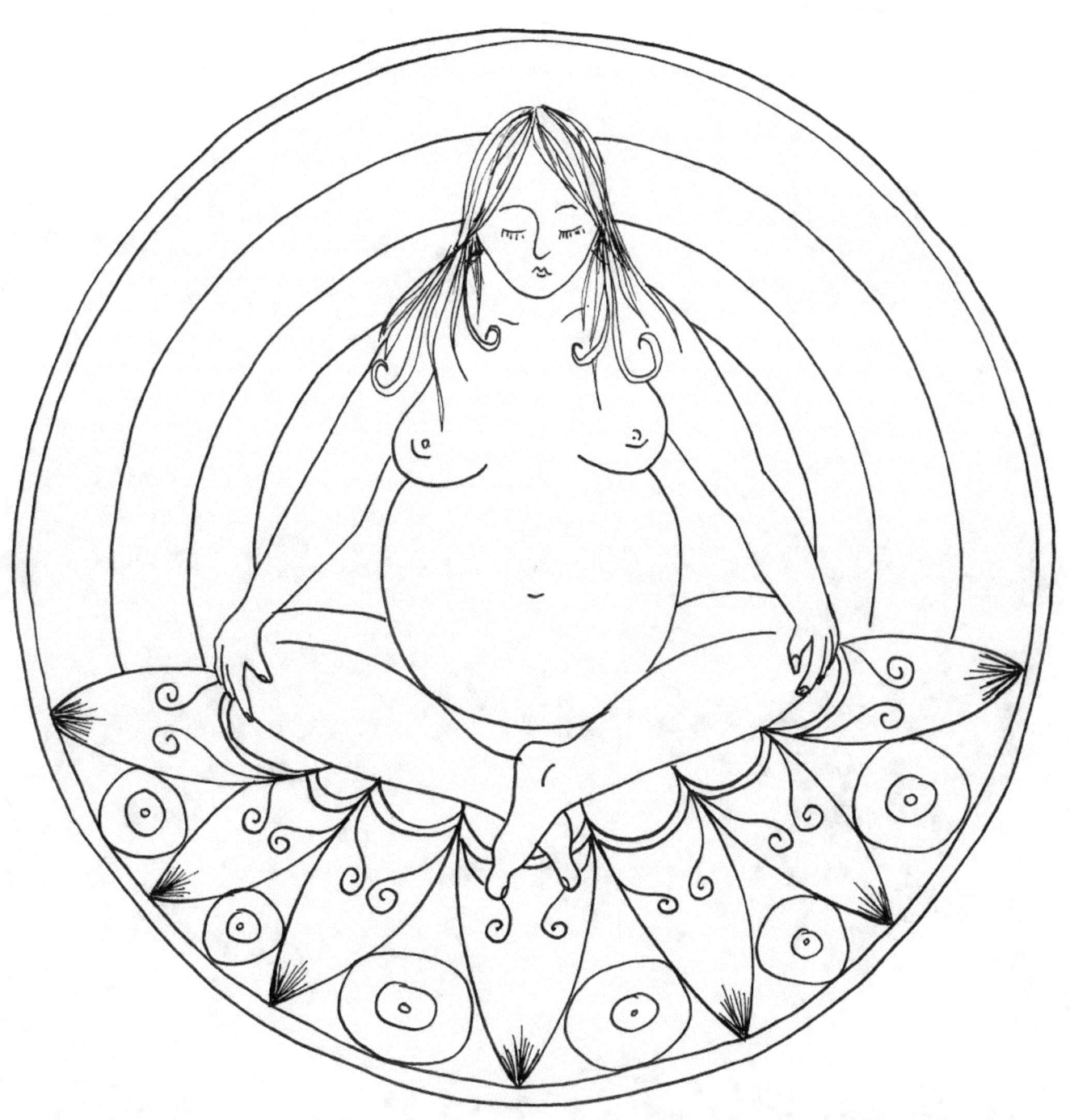

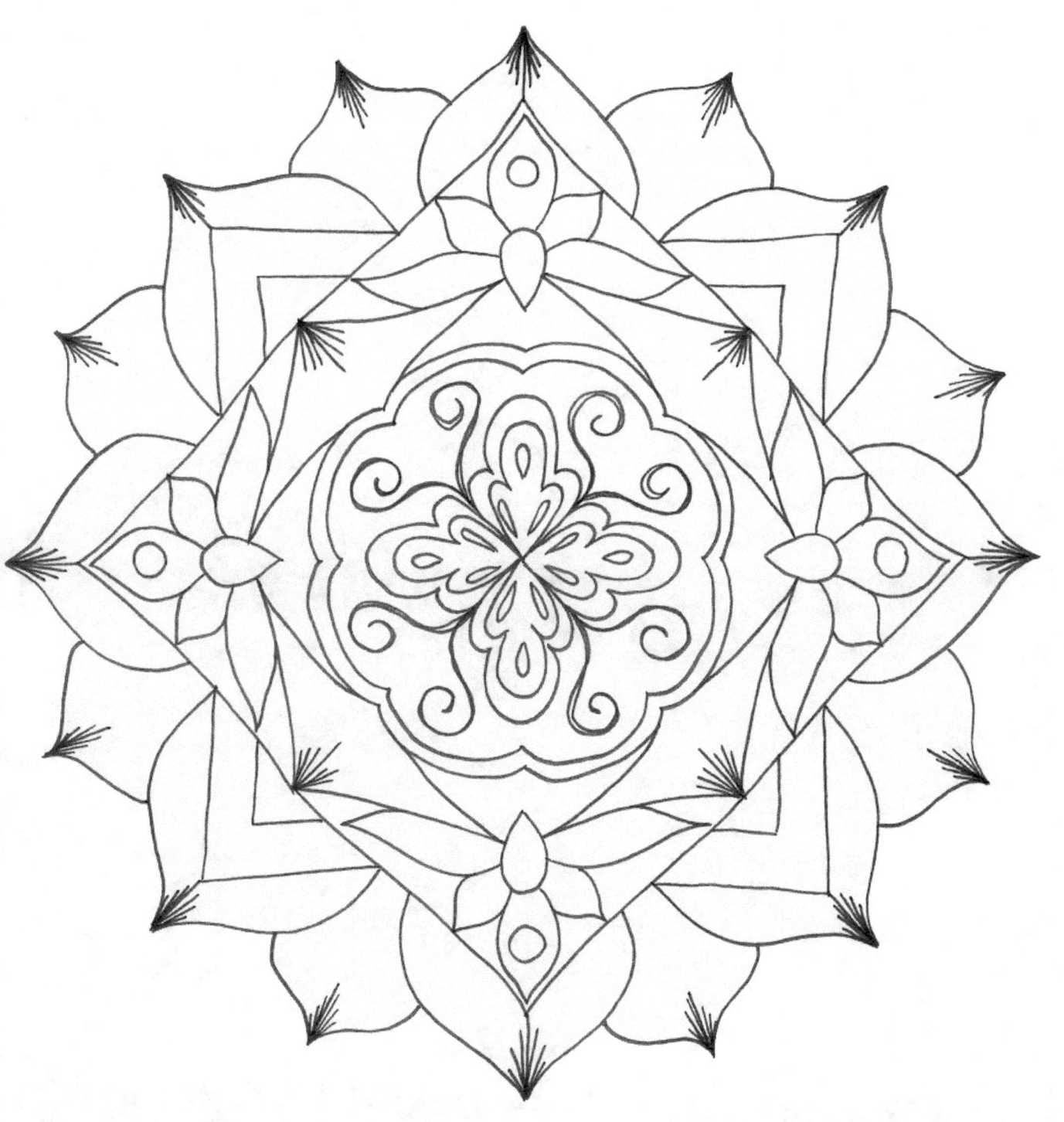

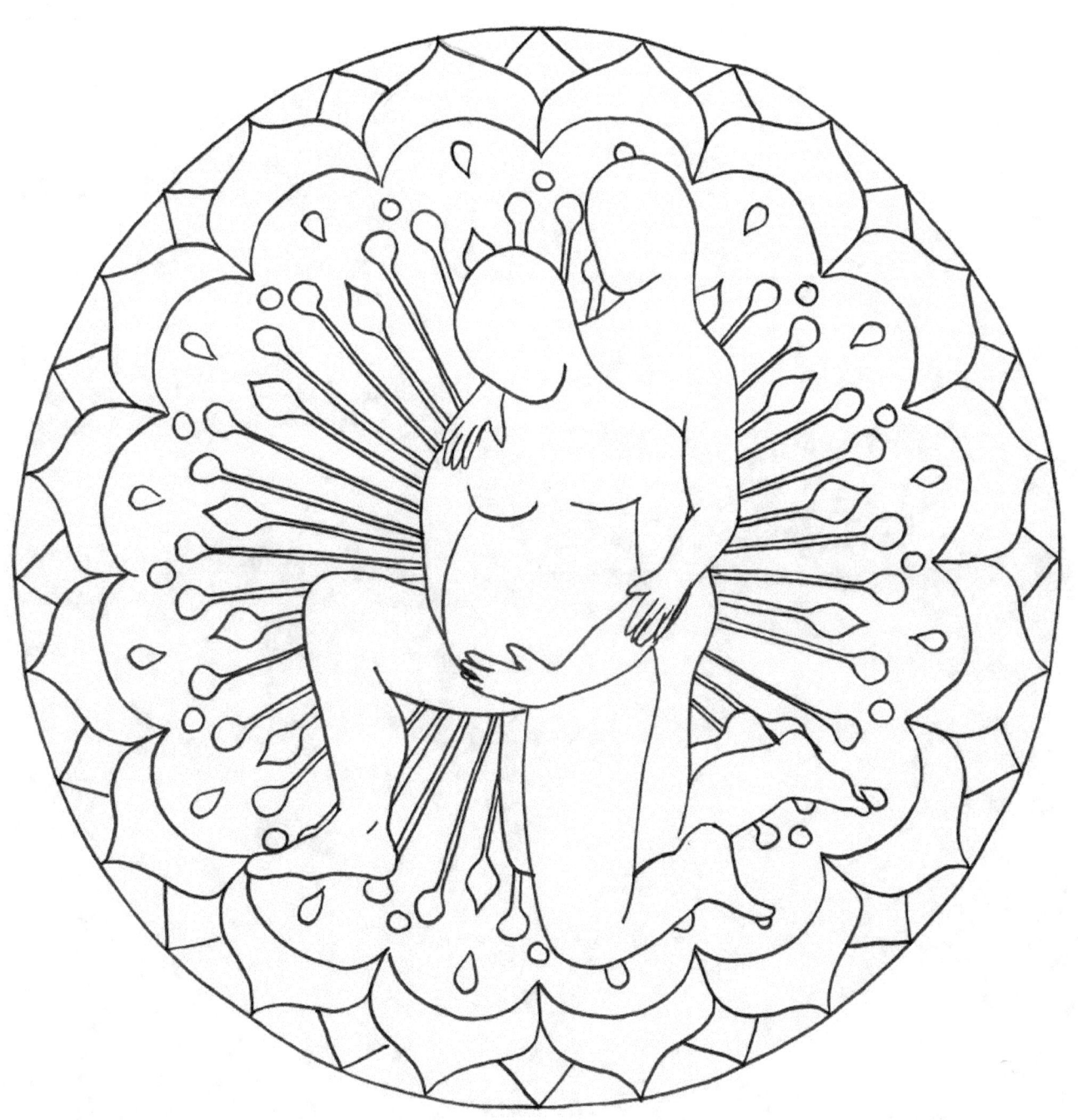

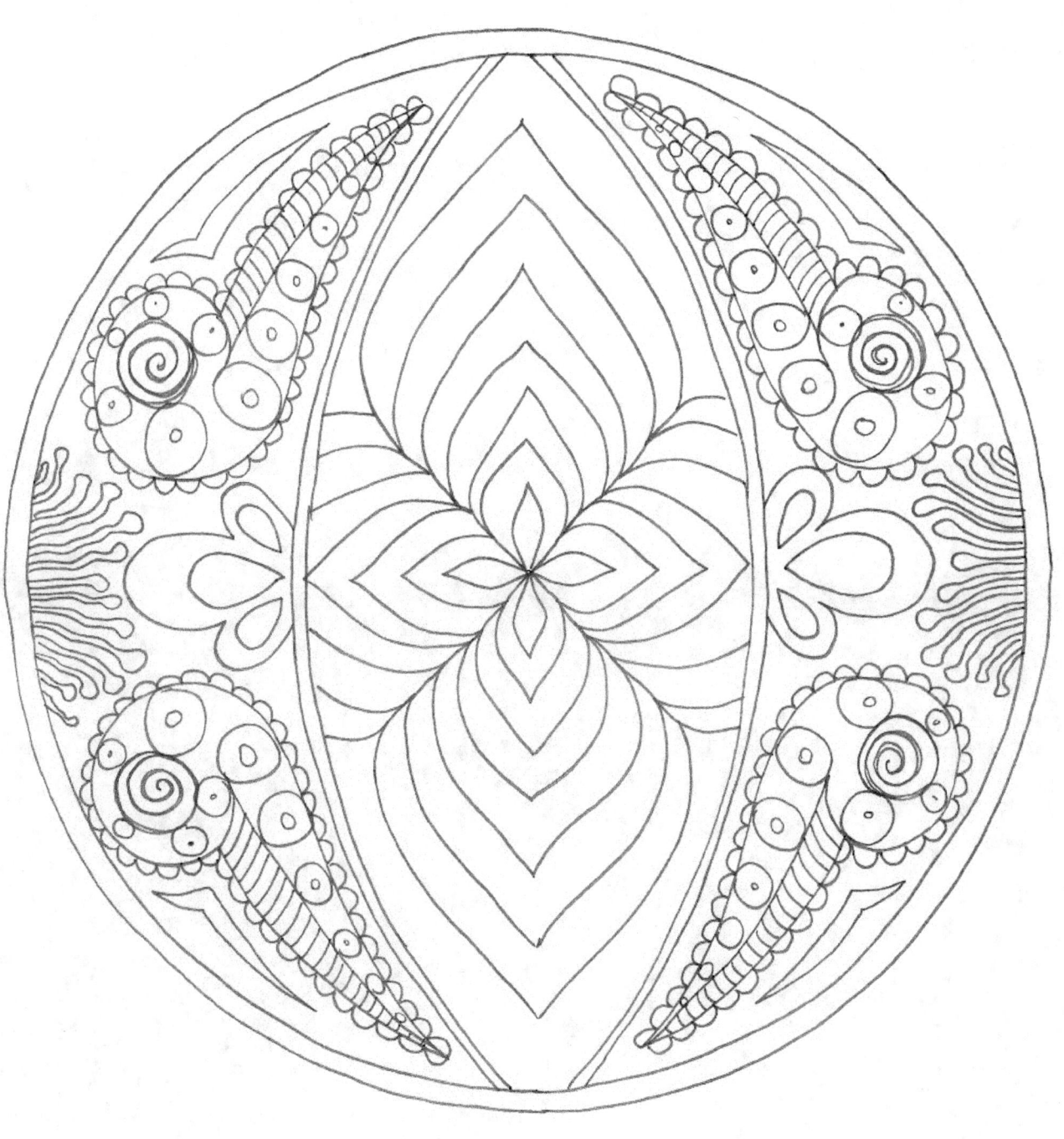

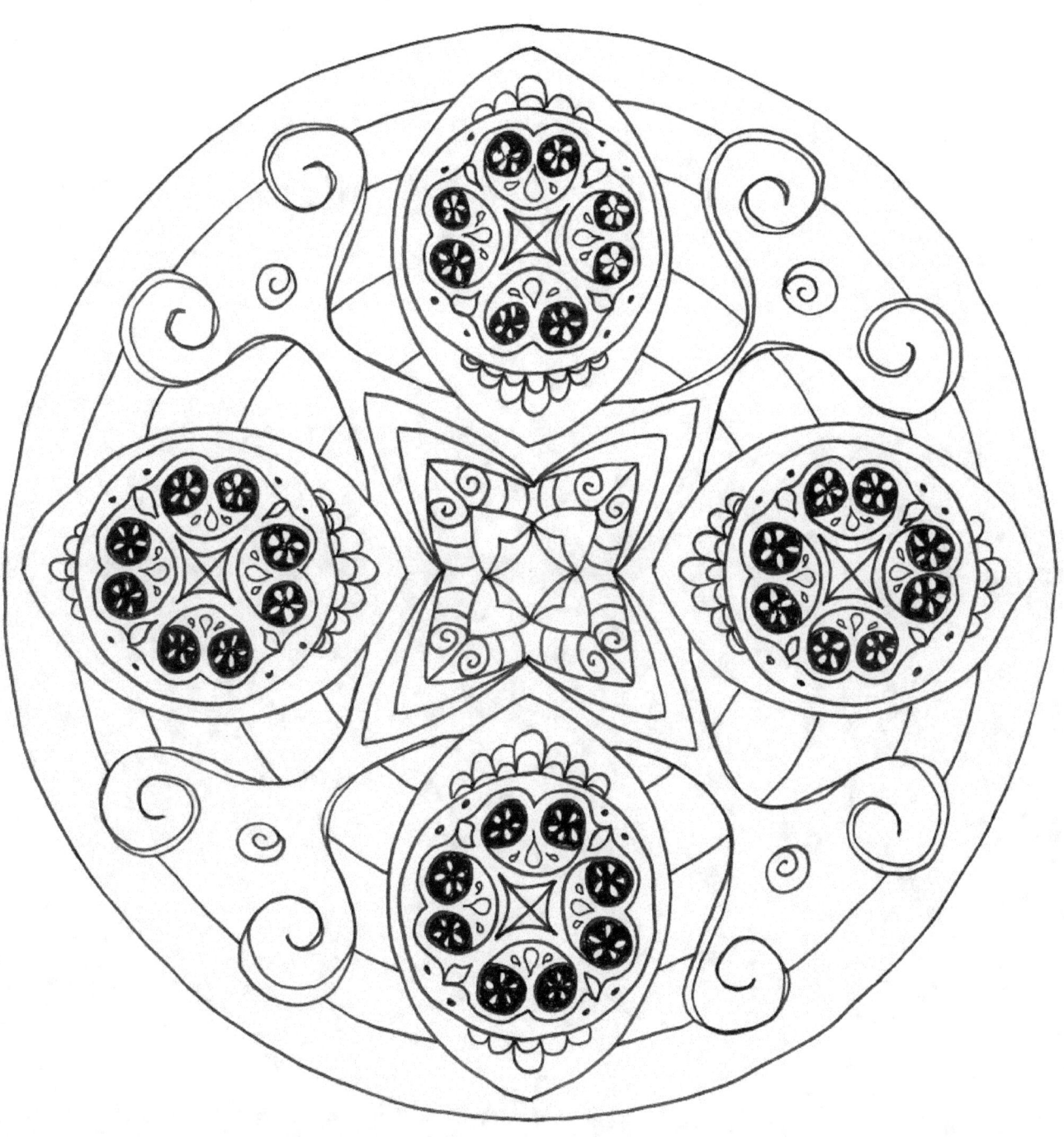

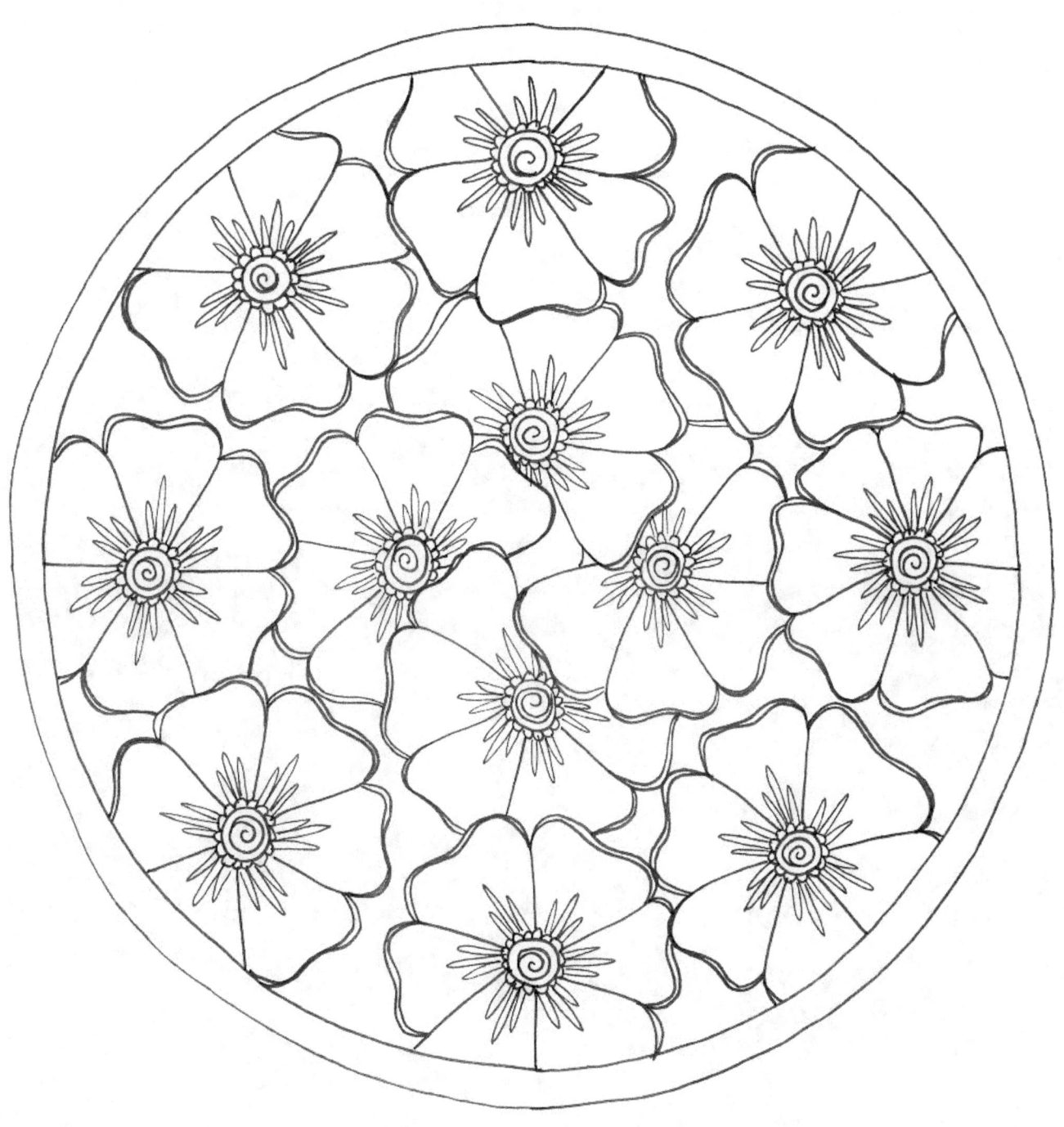

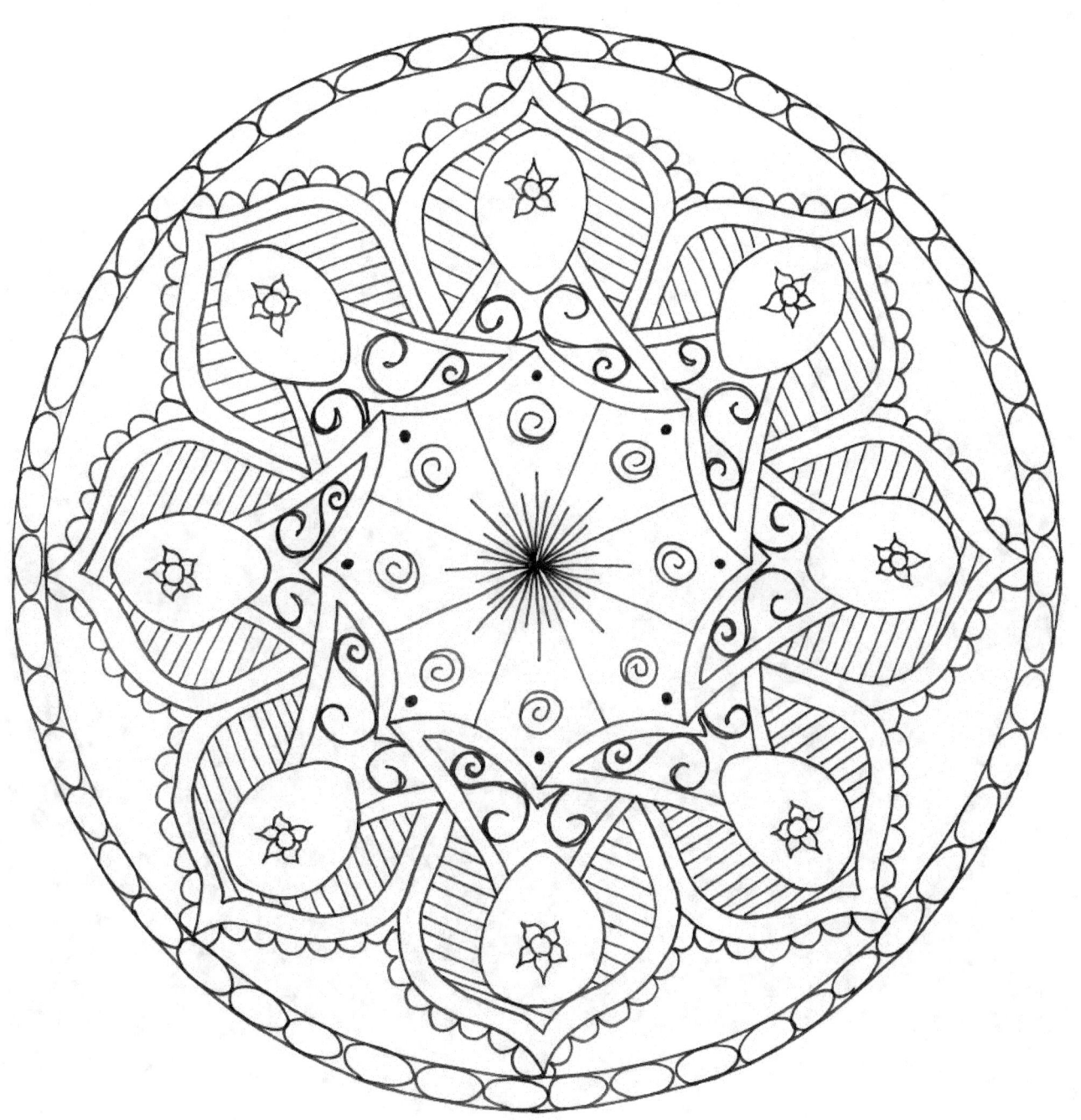

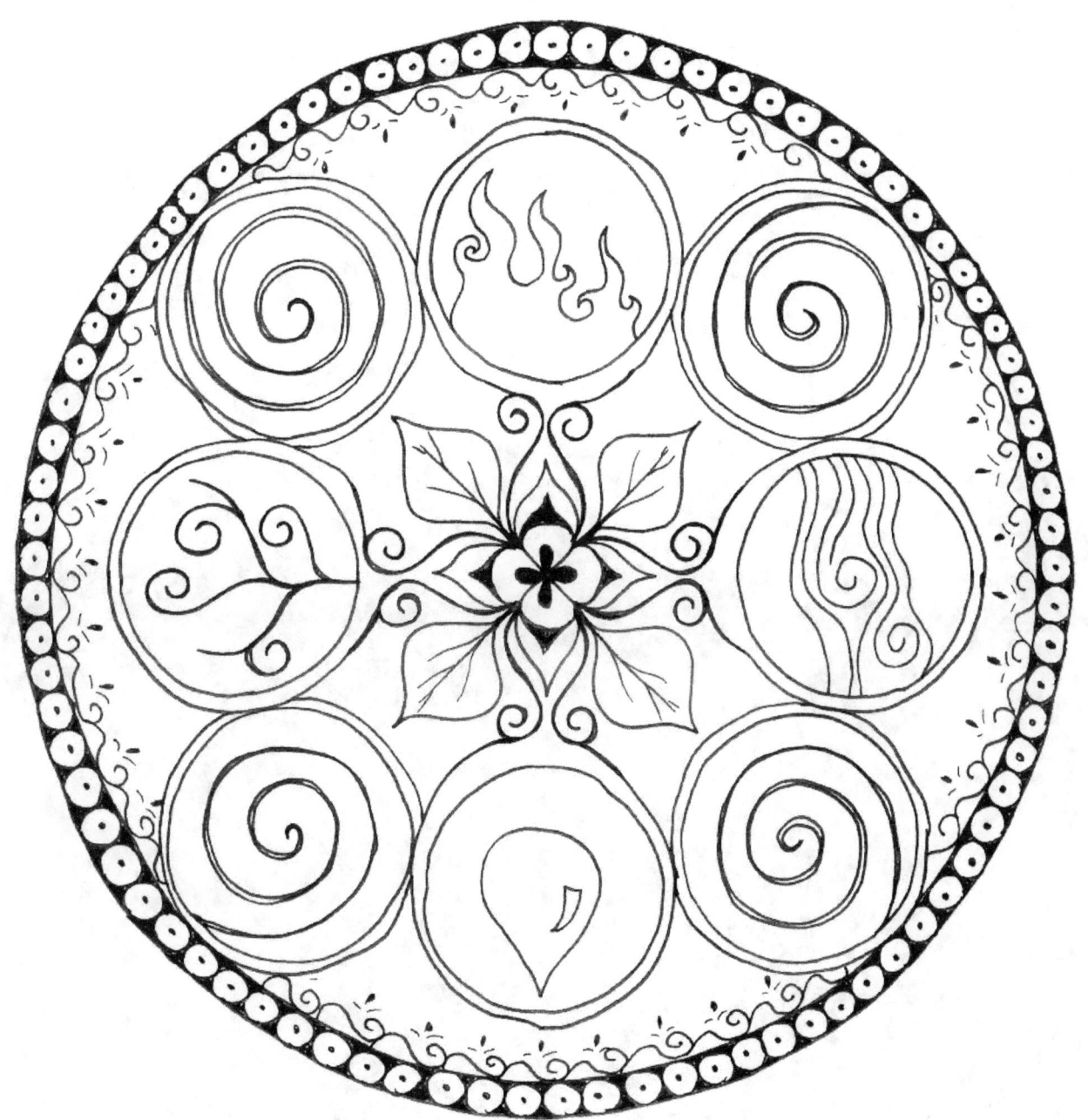

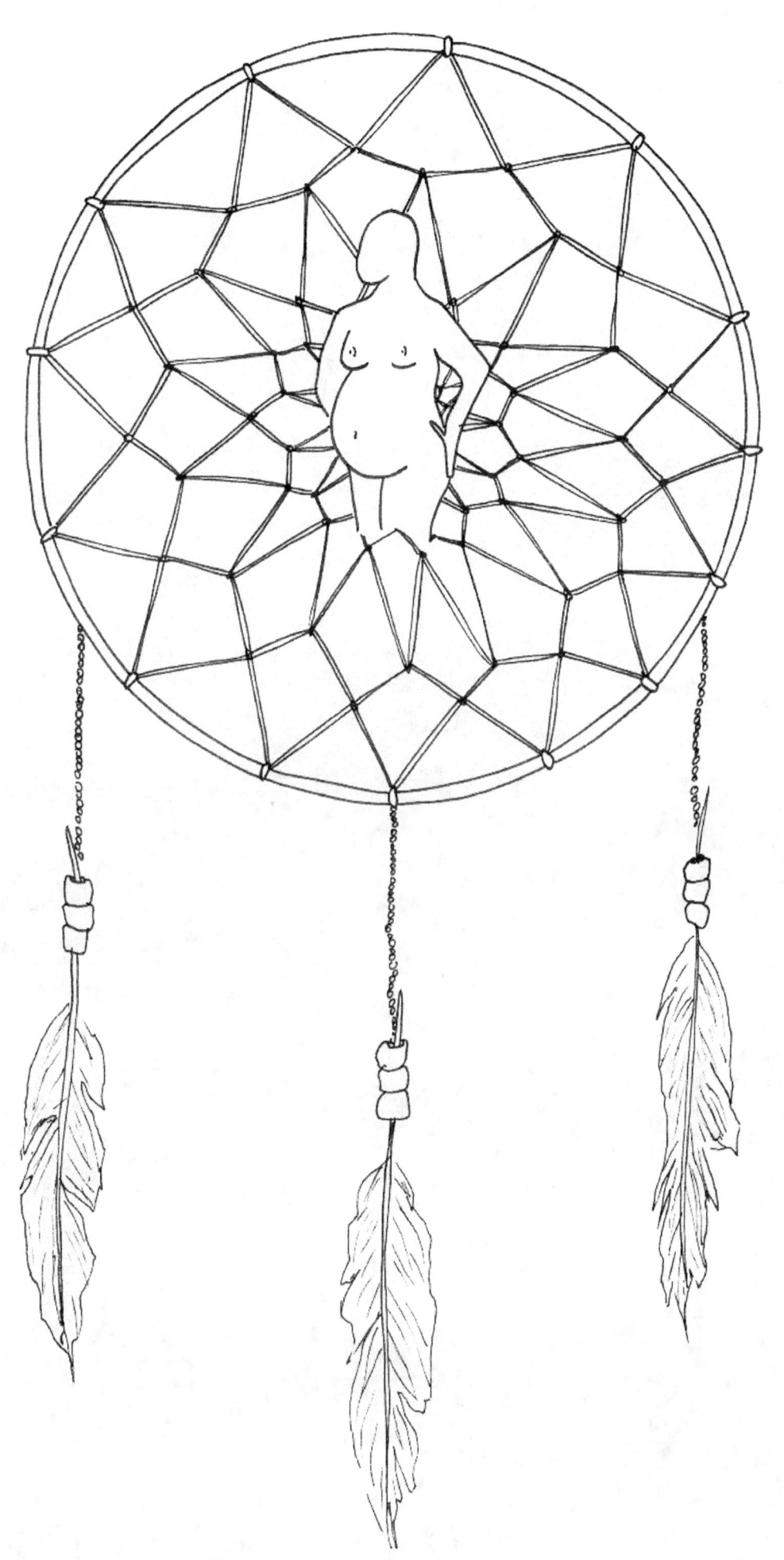

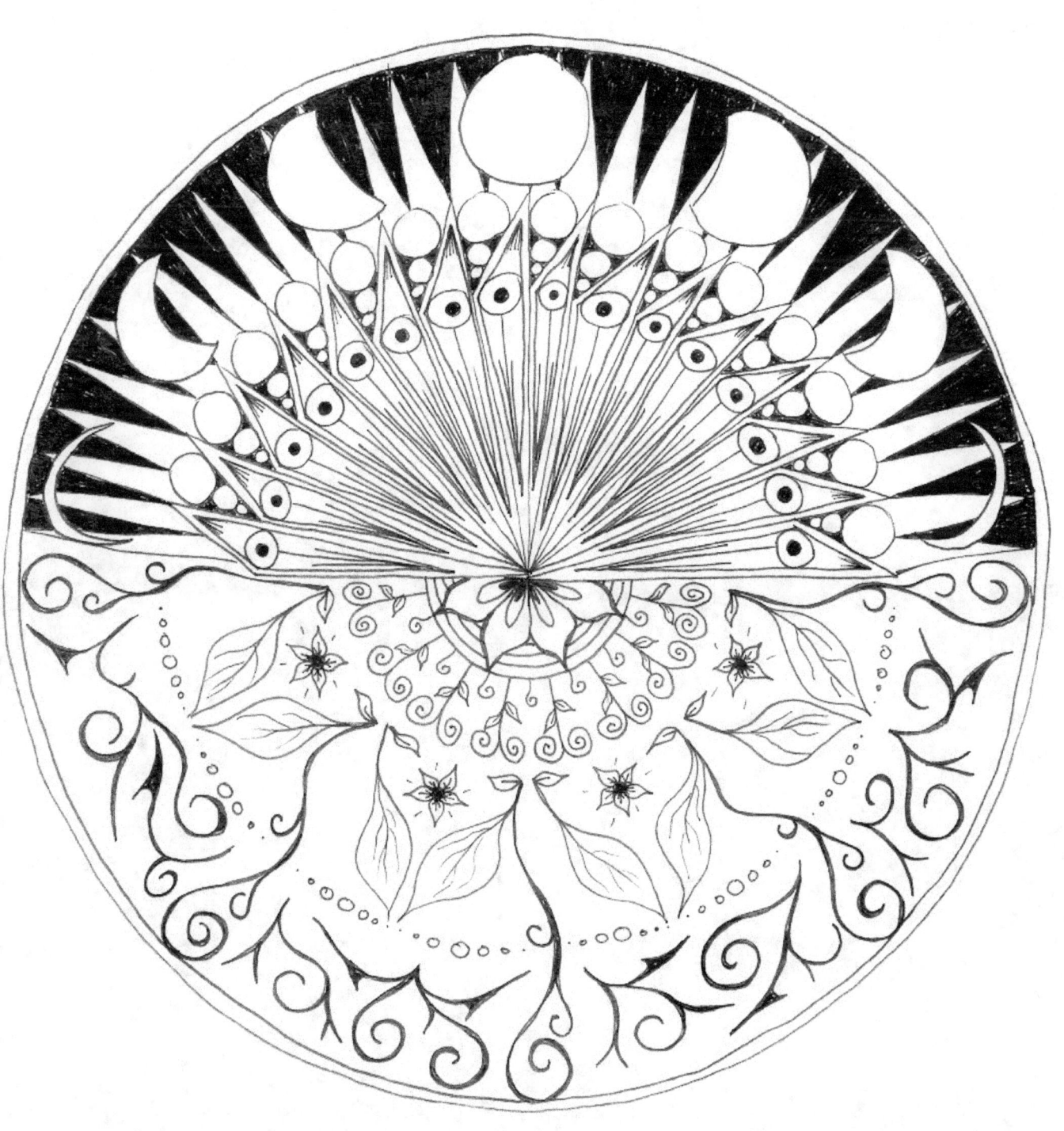

# About April

April is a woman of many talents including being a qualified Acupuncturist, Breastfeeding Counsellor, Birth Doula, Postnatal Doula, Childbirth Educator, and trainer for other birth professionals. She is also a mother of four, an artist, and musician.

While working with her acupuncture and birth clients she recognised an increasing need for patients time out, along with thinking about where they were going, and what was happening in their lives.

To fill this need April created a collection of colouring in books to help people to focus on the positives in their lives, and to take time out to rest their minds, while at the same time create beautiful artwork.

Visit her website www.nurturinglife.com.au to see what other books are also available.

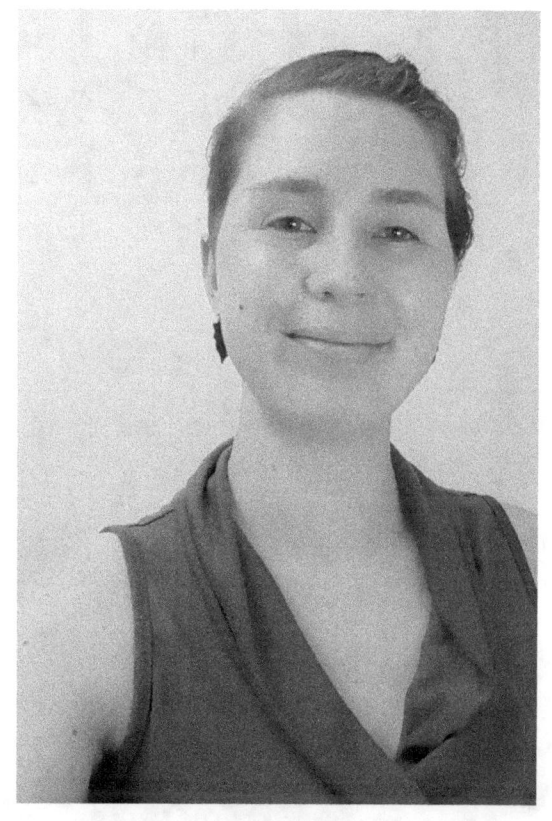

## Connect with me

Follow and tag me on Instagram:     @birthmandala

Please feel free to tag me or use #birthmandala in any images you post of finished coloured in pictures (or Instagram). I love seeing what everyone does with the pictures!

www.ingramcontent.com/pod-product-compliance
Lightning Source LLC
Chambersburg PA
CBHW081405170526
45166CB00010B/3209